Yours, Anne

The Life of Anne Frank

Yours, Anne

The Life of Anne Frank

Lois Metzger

SCHOLASTIC INC.

New York • Toronto • London • Auckland • Sydney
Mexico City • New Delhi • Hong Kong • Buenos Aires

PHOTO CREDITS

Front cover: (school picture) The Anne Frank House, Netherlands;
(house exterior) United States Holocaust Memorial Museum, Washington, D.C.

Back cover: (diary) The Anne Frank House, Netherlands

Insert: (in order of appearance) Hulton/GETTYIMAGES; Hulton/GETTYIMAGES; Hulton/GETTYIMAGES; The Anne Frank House, Netherlands; Hulton/GETTYIMAGES; Bettmann/CORBIS; The Anne Frank Center USA; The Anne Frank House, Netherlands; The Anne Frank House, Netherlands; The Anne Frank House, Netherlands; AP/Wide World Photos

ISBN 0-439-59099-X

Text copyright © 2004 by Lois Metzger

All rights reserved. Published by Scholastic Inc.

SCHOLASTIC and associated logos are trademarks and/or registered trademarks of Scholastic Inc.

12 11 10 9 8 7 6 5   4 5 6 7 8 9/0

Printed in the U.S.A.   40
First printing, March 2004

ACKNOWLEDGMENTS

Many thanks to Linda Ferreira, Rachel Lisberg, Steve Metzger, and Gina Shaw at Scholastic and Susan Cohen and Rebecca Sherman at Writers House. The following people read the book early on and I appreciate their insights and comments: Alexandra Garabedian, Michela Garabedian, Jacob Hiss, Rhoda Levine, Susan Logan, Nancy Novick, and Josh Silver. Also thanks to Margaret Zamos's sixth-graders at Friends Seminary in Manhattan who were part of the Anne Frank Book Club: Eric Brest, Uwingablye Cunningham, Joel Hochman, D'Meca Homer, Alec Lumey, Renata Mittnacht, Forrest Petterson, and Dillon Torcia.

Thanks to Tony Hiss — in a category by himself, as he always is.

CONTENTS

Yours, Anne

The Life of Anne Frank

PART ONE:

First Entry

❧

Anne Frank, one of the most famous writers who ever lived, died when she was only fifteen. People have called her the face of the Holocaust — the killing of six million Jews by Adolf Hitler's Nazi Germany during the Second World War. She could as accurately be called the voice of the Holocaust. Her diary, written when she was hiding from the Nazis, records what her family life was like, day by day, in a few small, damp rooms inside a lopsided old house in Amsterdam. More than that, her diary records, to perfection, the journey of a young girl turning into a young woman. This happened both lightning fast and infinitely slowly, during the endless hours of two years in hiding. Anne Frank, very ordinary in some ways and in others one of the most remarkable people in the world. Anne Frank — boy-crazy, superficial, self-involved, full of concern, furiously angry, deliriously happy, terrible at math, brilliant at writing, charming, very funny and with a wicked sense of humor, loving, thoughtful, despairing, hopeful, and unswervingly honest. She was a picture of opposites, "a bundle of contradictions," she called herself — in other words, a real teenager. And she started out as a real little girl.

§§

Anne grew up in Holland but was born in Germany on the morning of June 12, 1929. She didn't come into the world easily — or quietly. She had trouble breathing those first moments. And then she cried and cried. The nurse, who was tired after Anne's long, difficult birth, made a mistake and wrote down that Annelies Marie Frank was a boy.

Anne (pronounced Anna) became a fidgety baby. The summer was too hot and sticky for her. She fell asleep only after crying had worn her out and quieted down at night only when her father, Otto, went to her room and sang nursery songs to her. Anne's first smile was for him.

What a different baby! her mother, Edith, thought. Margot Betti, Anne's sister, three years older, had been so happy and calm, sleeping all night. Edith and Otto called her Little Angel. Margot's baby book was full of admiring details, describing her first steps, her first words. Anne's baby book had only the bare facts: "Has been screaming all night for the past six weeks."

So Anne was not an angelic baby — but she was very cute. Her ears stuck out. She had lots of black hair that Margot liked to touch. She had great big green eyes, dark eyebrows, long eyelashes. Otto said she loved attention and usually found a way to get it.

As a child, Anne was never afraid to speak up or speak out. When she was about four, she and her grandmother got on a crowded streetcar. Anne looked hard, gave everyone a piercing stare, and demanded, "Won't someone offer a seat to this old lady?"

Many adults found her rude, "saucy," spoiled. But Otto loved Anne's high spirits, and she made him laugh. She called her father Pim, her special name for him. Otto never knew where the name came from. He thought maybe it sounded like *père*, the French word for father. Just under six feet tall, Otto had a long face, a graying mustache, and very little hair on top of his head. He had endless patience for Anne's endless questions. She liked long, complicated answers, full of information, and if the answers were too skimpy she got mad. She was "a little rebel with a will of her own," Otto said, amazed and delighted by his daughter.

Otto told his two daughters stories about two sisters, the two Paulas, characters his mother had invented. Good Paula was perfect in every way. Bad Paula was nothing but trouble. Otto said the sisters were hidden and invisible — but you could hear them moving around if you held yourself very still.

Because Margot followed all the rules and Anne broke them, it might sound as though Margot was Good Paula and Anne was Bad Paula. But Anne came to realize that there was something like a Good Paula and a Bad Paula inside all of us, invisible, hiding, but present.

§§

The Franks lived in the German city of Frankfurt am Main, where Otto's family had lived since the 1600s. Otto, a businessman, loved his country, with its beautiful music and art and literature, and he was fiercely patriotic. Otto had been a German army officer in the First World War and had been awarded the Iron Cross. He was also Jewish, though not religious.

The family lived just outside the big city in a neighborhood that felt like a small town. Only four months after Anne was born, the New York stock market crashed, and the whole world entered the Great Depression. People lost jobs or struggled to keep them. When Anne was two, the family moved to a smaller, cheaper apartment. Adolf Hitler, head of Germany's Nazi party, blamed the Jews for the stock market crash and all the misery that followed. He called Jews "subhuman." Since Jews were hurt by the Depression as much as anyone else, Hitler sounded so crazy to Otto and Edith that they thought he would never be taken seriously.

In January 1933, Otto and Edith were out visiting friends when they heard the news: Hitler had just been elected chancellor, or prime minister, of Germany. Edith looked as if she had turned to stone. For the past year, groups of Nazis had been marching in the streets, singing songs about killing Jews. Now these people were in charge of the government.

Things changed fast. By April, armed Nazis forced people away from Jewish shops and businesses. New laws made it illegal for Jews to work in government or as teachers. Now Margot and other Jewish students had to sit in the back of the classroom, away from the "pure" Germans. By May, books by Jewish authors were burned in the streets. People who spoke out against Hitler were instantly put in jail. When the jails got too full, huge numbers of prisoners were then confined or "concentrated" into small holding camps in the countryside. These places were called concentration camps.

It was at this time that Otto Frank decided to leave Germany, the home his family had known for centuries, the country he had been willing to die for.

§

One spring day in 1934, when Anne was almost five, her mother took her to a grocery store in Amsterdam, Holland's biggest city. While buying butter and milk, Edith started to talk to a woman who also had her daughter next to her. What a coincidence! each said to the other. Both daughters were the same age. Both families were German and Jewish and had only recently arrived in Holland. Most amazing of all, they were next-door neighbors in an area of South Amsterdam called the River Quarter. The other girl was tall and thin and had brown hair in tight curls. She and Anne just looked at each other.

A few days later, Anne went to school for the first time. Edith was afraid that Anne would throw a fit and demand to be taken home. But Anne noticed the girl from the store there. The girl headed straight for Anne — and Anne fell into her arms. That was how Hanneli Elisabeth Goslar became Anne's first friend in Holland.

§§

Holland, a small, low-to-the-ground country between France and Germany on the edge of the North Sea, had stayed out of the First World War. As a neutral country, it had never been invaded by the British, the French, or even by the Germans. Otto was counting on this. Should there ever be another war, he was sure that Holland would again be a place of safety.

Then and now, life in Amsterdam was all about water and sky. The city has 150 canals linked by 1,300 bridges. Narrow houses are built right at the water's edge, so you can see their shimmery reflections. In this way, the city seems doubled.

Although Anne lived in a modern part of Amsterdam, she noticed that many of the houses in the Old City, downtown, leaned to the left or right. This was because the centuries-old piles they were built on, which had been pounded down through forty feet of marshy soil to a hard layer of sand, were starting to rot. (A thousand years ago, Amsterdam was just a swamp.) The leaning houses stood next to one another in rows, looking like dominoes about to fall. These old houses were full of unexpected creaks as they settled. Cooking in a leaning house was always tricky. Frying pans with scrambled eggs had to be watched carefully, or the eggs might spill out.

Because Amsterdam — and all of Holland — was flat as a board and the buildings not much higher than five stories (a twelve-story tower was called a skyscraper), the sky was everywhere, all the time. And it could be spectacular. Heavy dark-gray clouds with only glimpses of pale blue. Or swirly white clouds with light streaming through them, right next to thick, black, billowing clouds about to burst. Or a sky that looked cut in half with a pencil line — unbroken dark clouds on one side, blue on the other, covering half the ground in darkness and bathing the other half in light. In winter the air smelled like ice and the sky was white; in the chilly drizzle of summer, the sky could look yellow. Fog sometimes blotted out sunlight for days. Low ash-colored clouds at dusk gave the illusion of mountains in the distance.

For Anne, Holland was just right. Like her, the country was lively and friendly. Her neighborhood was more like a suburb, with wide streets and identical five-story light-brown brick apartment houses with white shutters and balconies in back. The housing complex was brand-new, and because there was much construction still going on there were always huge sandpiles to play in. The Franks' apartment, on the third floor, with its many books, dark shiny antiques, and a grandfather clock that needed winding every three or four weeks, was big enough to have an extra room they could rent to earn extra money. Anne liked to lean out the front window, listen to church bells, and watch people gather to talk and ride by on their black bicycles. The flat land of Holland was ideal for bike riding. She could also see children play hoops, rolling what looked like hula hoops by pushing them with sticks.

Anne turned five on June 12, 1934, and celebrated with a party in her new home with her new friends. There was Hanneli, of course, and Susanne Ledermann, the younger sister of Margot's friend Barbara. Susanne was also German and Jewish. Anne called her Sanne (which rhymed with Anna). These three were called Anne, Hanne, Sanne.

§♦

For seven years, Anne went to a nearby elementary school that had its own ideas on how children could learn. The school didn't push everyone to read, write, or do math at the same time. Instead, children could read at their own pace, follow their own interests, and work by themselves or with one another.

This, too, was just right for Anne, who wasn't crazy about anyone telling her what to do or how to do it. She liked building blocks and gardening and drawing and especially admired a girl named Kitty, who drew beautifully. Math was impossible, and reading didn't come easily. When Anne was a little older, Edith complained in a letter, "Anne is learning to read *with great difficulty*." But later on Anne became, as she herself said, "mad on books and reading."

In a city full of bikes and so few cars, it was safe to play in the streets. Under the amazing cloudy skies, children played hide-and-seek, marbles, stickball, jump rope, went roller-skating, and rolled hoops. Anne couldn't do cartwheels, something the other girls did, just as she couldn't play tennis or row a boat. She had a bad shoulder that sometimes popped out of its socket.

Margot went to a different, more traditional school because Edith and Otto thought the freedom of Anne's school wouldn't be good for her. Margot's grades were perfect. She and her friend Barbara would ride their bikes together, and people just stared at these two beautiful girls. Margot's lush dark hair blew in the breeze; Barbara was blond and blue-eyed. They were called Snow White and Rose Red.

Margot and Edith were close, but from an early age Anne saw that she and her mother were "exact opposites in everything," as she later put it. Anne loved the spotlight. Edith preferred the shadows. In Holland, Anne felt herself moving further away from her mother. Edith seemed sad and tired and always looked older than her age because she wore her dark hair parted in the middle and tucked into a bun at the back of her neck. For Edith, Germany was still home. She complained that Dutch chocolate wasn't nearly as good as German chocolate, that Dutch clothing wasn't nearly as well made. She tried studying Dutch with a tutor but gave up after only two lessons, and instead picked up the language in bits and pieces. It bothered Anne that her mother didn't just fall into the arms of Holland, the way Anne had done with Hanneli.

৯৳

Anne's friends liked the Franks' home better than their own. You got to eat rolls covered in cream cheese and shaved chocolate and drink real bottled milk, not milk you filled up in your own jar at the grocery store. Otto was always a big part of any visit. He did something with a beer glass — tipping it back, back, back until it almost spilled. That always made Hanneli laugh. And Otto was infinitely patient with Anne. Hanneli watched as Anne, sometimes fighting even when she didn't know what she was fighting about, received in return only gentle words from her father. Edith, on the other hand, tried to get Anne to straighten up.

She must sit at the table to drink her hot chocolate! Edith would say.

Anne only got angry and said, no, never!

And Otto would say, it's all right, let her sit where she likes.

Like all of Anne's friends, Hanneli thought Otto was the perfect father.

A year after the Franks left Germany, the Nazis passed laws that protected "German blood" from "alien blood." You couldn't marry somebody who wasn't Jewish. Jewish lawyers could only have Jewish clients. Jewish doctors could only have Jewish patients. Also, Jews could no longer vote.

There was far worse to come. On November 9, 1938, Nazis ransacked every city in Germany and Austria, destroying Jewish stores and burning synagogues. This was called *Kristallnacht* or Night of Broken Glass because, the Nazis said, the broken glass from shattered windows shone as beautifully as crystal. Afterward, tens of thousands of Jews were sent to concentration camps.

Anne's parents didn't want her to know about such things, even though Edith's brother had been arrested after *Kristallnacht*. "Something awful" had happened to Uncle Walter, Anne told her friends, but that was all she knew. On Saturday afternoons, Edith and Otto always had friends over for coffee. But they stopped talking politics when Anne or Margot was around. Besides, Otto felt that better times might lie ahead. *Kristallnacht*, he said, was like "the high fever of an illness" — the sickness that had taken hold of Germany might have peaked and Germany could now recover.

§§

Otto Frank threw himself into his work. He ran the Opekta Company, which made pectin, something you could stir into ground-up fruit to make it gel. The company slogan was "Jams and Jellies in 10 Minutes." His secretary was a young woman named Hermine Santrouschitz, called Miep (pronounced Meep). Short, round-faced, with ash-blond hair, Miep had been born in Austria. There had been a terrible shortage of food in Austria during and after the First World War. As a child, Miep was "wasting away," she said. "My legs were sticks. . . . My teeth were soft."

Eleven-year-old Miep came to Holland as part of a special program for hungry Austrian children. To take more with her, she wore layers of clothing on her journey. She was only supposed to stay for three months, but when the time was up, she stayed on in Holland for another three months, and then another and another. Like Anne, Miep loved her new country for its *gezellig* — its coziness — which made the whole place feel like a big friendly village. Miep never returned to Austria, except for short visits, which made her realize that she had become "Dutch through and through."

Miep and Anne had many other things in common. Anne had health problems of her own. She was said to have a heart condition, and she had a fever that kept coming back. Edith remarked of her, "The nervous little thing needs to have plenty of rest." Anne's nickname was *Zartlein* — Fragile One. Edith kept Anne out of school and in bed for weeks. Anne hated just lying around. At school, she never took part in gym, because of her shoulder. But it didn't hurt when it popped out of its socket. She would pop it out on purpose for her friends. Hanneli said it made a sound — *clack, clack, clack* — and that Anne "thought that it was great fun to have the other children watch and burst out laughing."

Miep kept a diary when she was a teenager, writing down her most private thoughts and feelings. "I did all this in secret, for myself only, not for discussion," she said. "I had a deep longing for an understanding of life." But later, embarrassed that someday someone might find it and read it, she tore the whole thing up. Anne began writing a diary on her thirteenth birthday. She recorded an amazing range of thought, depth of feeling, and a many-layered understanding of life. Her diary survives only because Miep saved it. Anne's diary, first published two years after her death, has so far sold twenty-five million copies in nearly seventy languages.

§§

The first time Miep saw her, Anne was four and shy and wearing a fluffy snow-white fur coat. *Here's the kind of child I'd like to have someday,* flashed into Miep's mind. Miep was sometimes invited to the Franks' home and watched the children grow. It touched Miep's heart, the way eight-year-old Anne's socks kept slouching at her thin ankles. Miep noticed her "electric gray-green eyes with green flecks," so deep set they could look shrouded in shadow. She admired Anne and Margot's glossy dark hair, always just washed, cut below the ears, parted on the side, held in place by barrettes. Margot, almost a teenager, was growing even more beautiful. Unlike Anne, she sat ladylike, back straight, hands folded in her lap, and kept her thoughts to herself.

Miep said that Anne, at nine, had "quite a personality." She was always going on and on about her many friends as though "each were her best and only friend." Anne loved to talk — and talk and talk. She spoke fast in a high-pitched voice, her words coming out all in a rush. She took over conversations. She was called a know-it-all (and she hated to be criticized). She got in trouble at school for talking so much.

But Anne's talents also got noticed at school. When children were asked to write plays, Anne bubbled over with ideas. She also got the best parts in these plays. She was a terrific mimic, perfectly capturing a cat's meow, or one of her friends, or her own teacher scolding her for talking too much. Miep said Anne was "crazy about the movies." Anne talked about becoming a movie star.

Anne also liked history, Greek mythology, cats, dogs, vacations at the sea or bicycling in the country, swimming (her favorite sport), skating (her second favorite), sunbathing on her roof, ice-cream parlors, collecting postcards of movie stars, and clowning around to get laughs. Miep noticed changes in the preteen Anne, how her thin legs and arms seemed almost too long for her body. But Anne still loved being the baby in the family, especially in her father's eyes.

§§

On September 1, 1939, when Anne was ten, Hitler invaded Poland. England and France demanded that Hitler pull back. When he refused, they declared war on Germany. The Second World War had begun. Hitler's victory over Poland was startlingly fast, but ·for months after that nothing much happened. Some people starting calling it the Phony War. But Margot wrote to a pen pal in America, "We never feel safe."

On Friday, May 10, 1940, Germany invaded Holland.

On the radio, the queen of Holland said the Dutch army "would not give up without a fight." But the Polish army had put up a fight, too. Anne hated the many air-raid sirens and the bombs at night that made her cry and run to her father. She got upset and angry when Holland surrendered five days later.

In many ways, Anne's life continued much as it had before. On Sundays, she enjoyed visiting her father's large new office in the Old City, which he moved into in December. She often took Hanneli along. They typed letters to each other in the office and, as Hanneli remembered, got "the chance to play our favorite game: telephoning from one room to another. That was quite an adventure."

Otto's office was right on the once elegant ancient Prinsengracht, the Prince's Canal, created more than three hundred years earlier when Amsterdam had been the most important port in the world. The office was actually two houses connected by a narrow passageway — a four-story front house and a five-story back house. Together, these buildings at 263 Prinsengracht — which in 1940 were just an office and a warehouse — later became a great landmark of the world. They are now a museum, the Anne Frank House, which gets more than 800,000 visitors a year.

§§

The front house was tall and narrow and made of dark-red brick with vast, enormous windows, and it leaned against the other houses on the street. It had been built back in the 1600s; the back house was a hundred years younger. There was a big connected warehouse on the ground floor of both houses. It was used for pectin and for herbs and spices that were part of a new meat-seasonings business Otto had started up a couple of years earlier. Above the warehouse in the front house were offices, and on the floor above were supplies. In the back house, Otto kept his own office and a kitchen. Both buildings had a lot of empty space, with small rooms on the top floors.

Behind the back house was a big courtyard garden with an enormous old chestnut tree. A block away was the Westerkerk or West Church, the city's most beautiful church, as old as the neighborhood itself. The church's tower, the Westertoren or the West Tower, was the city's tallest, 280 feet high, and it had the heaviest bell, at eight and a half tons. The tower had a gold-blue-and-red crown and weather vane, a perfect gold circle of a clock with roman numerals, and forty-eight booming bells that loudly rang out the time.

Besides Miep, about ten other people worked at 263 Prinsengracht, some only part-time. Hermann van Pels was said to have a perfect nose for herbs and spices. Like the Franks, Hermann van Pels had come to Amsterdam from Germany, along with his wife, Auguste (called Gusti), and their son, Peter, who was two and a half years older than Anne. Hermann liked to tell loud, long jokes. Otto considered Hermann his partner. Other office workers included Bep Voskuijl, a young typist; Johannes Kleiman, a bookkeeper; and Victor Gustav Kugler, Otto's right-hand man.

§§

Anne "had a lot of friends," Hanneli said years later. "She had more boys as friends than girls. . . . Boys really liked her. And she always liked it a lot when all the boys paid attention to her." Hanneli called her "spicy" and said, "She had long hair and she was always fussing with it. Her hair kept her busy all the time." Miep said that now Anne's "chatter" was full of talk about "the opposite sex."

But just when Anne was getting noticed and enjoying all the attention, Jews throughout Holland were in effect being erased. "Inch by inch" was how it felt, remembered Hanneli. In August 1940, all German Jews had to register their names at an Office of Resident Foreigners. Otto registered on behalf of the family.

As of the following January, Jews could no longer

go to the movies, and Anne adored movies. Otto and Edith went out of their way for her, renting movies and projectors so their home could be a movie theater. Anne made the shows extra special, printing out invitations and tickets for her friends. WITHOUT THIS CARD — NO ENTRY! one of them said at the top, and then, the date: MARCH 1, SUNDAY, 1:00. PLEASE INFORM IN TIME, it said below. Ticket holders were also given an assigned seat: ROW 2, SEAT 2.

A Dutch group called the NSB — the Dutch Nazi party — now had 100,000 members. But most of the Dutch supported the Jews, some risking their own lives to do so. When an NSB man was murdered in February 1941, the Germans arrested four hundred fifty Jews, who were never seen again. To protest the arrests, thousands of Dutch workers went on strike for two days. Everything stopped — all the streetcars and canal boats — and shops and factories and businesses closed. It gave a tremendous lift to the people of Amsterdam, and the strike is still remembered as the Day Beyond Praise.

"We're not likely to get sunburned, because we can't go to the swimming pool," Anne wrote with sly humor to her grandmother. At the end of May, just when the weather was turning hot, Jews had been banned from beaches and swimming pools.

Otto knew it was only a matter of time before Jews could no longer own businesses. Over several months, he transferred his companies to his coworkers Victor Kugler and Johannes Kleiman. That way, even though Otto still ran things, the businesses now officially had non-Jewish owners.

When it was time to go to school in the fall, Anne was told she had to repeat last year's grade. Because of health problems she'd missed many days and was especially behind in math. But then came another new law, and suddenly Jewish children could not go to school with non-Jewish children. This was announced only after classes had already begun, so the Jewish children — about half of Anne's class — were very publicly kicked out.

Otto took Anne to the country for a few days to try to make her feel better. While they were away, more new laws for Jews were announced.

You had to have a large black *J* printed on your identity card.

You could not keep pigeons. (Some people found this odd.)

You could not visit parks, zoos, cafés, restaurants, concert halls, coffeehouses, hotels, theaters, libraries.

JEWS FORBIDDEN signs were now everywhere. Some said NO DOGS OR JEWS. Hanneli's parents tried to make the best of it, saying things like, "If that's all, we can bear it. If we can't go to a concert — have chamber music at home."

Despite the best efforts of the grown-ups, Jewish children had to face the fact that their world was shrinking and that they, too, were on their way to becoming, as the Germans put it, "nonpersons."

In a misty, rainy October, Anne, who didn't have to repeat the grade after all, began attending the Jewish Secondary School — all Jewish children, all Jewish teachers — in a building that until then had been a woodworking plant. That October, Anne also got a small black cat she adored. She named the cat Moortje, which means Little Blackie.

She made a new best friend, Jacqueline van Maarsen, called Jacque (pronounced Jack-kay), a girl with enormous blue eyes, a girl who seemed sophisticated. Anne could talk to Jacque about boys, and Jacque had answers to Anne's many questions.

Anne loved knowing things and instantly showing off what she knew. "God knows everything, but Anne knows everything better," Hanneli's mother used to say with affection.

At the end of April 1942, Jews had to purchase six-pointed yellow cloth patches as big as a fist, with JOOD (Jew) printed in black letters. All Jews over six years old had to wear these Jewish stars sewn to coats and dresses and placed exactly on the left side above the heart. Whenever a Jew went outside, even if it was only to the balcony, the stars had to be visible. Miep remembered that in one neighborhood known as the Jewish Quarter there were so many of these stars it was laughingly called Hollywood.

ॐ

Anne Frank became a teenager on Friday, June 12, 1942. On the cold morning of her thirteenth birthday, she popped out of bed at six o'clock, knowing there would be presents, knowing there would be one in particular, something she'd picked out herself several days earlier at a bookstore with her father.

A diary.

A thick, nearly square autograph book with a plaid cloth cover and an oval snap clasp. The plaid was bold and cheerful, with crisscrosses of orange, white, and gray, and just a touch of pale green.

At school, Anne had always shielded her writing with her hand, Hanneli said, so no one could see what she was up to. "I thought that she was writing entire books," Hanneli said.

Now, as a teenager, Anne had an entire book to write in — a real all-to-herself diary.

That chilly morning, Hanneli and Anne walked to school together under thick gray clouds sweeping across the sky. They had to walk, because Jews were no longer allowed on the streetcars or even to ride their own bikes. That very day still more restrictions were announced for Jews.

You could only go shopping between three and five in the afternoon, and only in Jewish shops.

You had to stay indoors every night between eight P.M. and six the next morning.

You were not allowed to take photographs, but pictures could be taken of you.

You could not play any sport at all, including rowing and fishing.

Anne's friend Jacque said she was afraid to do anything because it probably wasn't allowed.

Anne had baked birthday cookies for her teachers and classmates, which she handed out at recess. She got to choose the game her whole class would play (volleyball), and they circled around her to sing "Happy Birthday."

At her party a couple of days later, she liked her many presents — roses, a blue blouse, a puzzle, cold cream, and books — and the fact that so many different people had thought about her on her birthday, including Peter van Pels, the son of Otto's partner, Hermann. Peter gave her a chocolate bar.

Her first entry in her favorite present, the diary, was written on her birthday: "I hope I will be able to confide everything to you, as I have never been able to confide in anyone, and I hope you will be a great source of comfort and support."

§§

Anne's diary entries over the next few weeks got longer and more confiding, even while she wondered whether anyone, including herself, would ever want to read about what was going on inside the mind of a thirteen-year-old. She always wrote with a fountain pen her grandmother had given her on her ninth birthday, holding it in a strange grip, between her index and middle fingers. Ink from the pen turned her fingers gray-blue.

What is known today about Anne Frank changes dramatically on her thirteenth birthday. Before then, she can be seen only from the outside, through the memories of other people. Now, in the diary, she is speaking for herself, about herself, in a chatty, funny, energetic, all-wrapped-up-in-herself voice.

"I've never had a real friend," Anne wrote on June 15. "At first I thought Jacque would be one, but I was badly mistaken." This was so like Anne, completely crazy about her friends one moment and in the next ready to give up on them. But even when upset with Jacque, she begged to sleep over at her house. She got jealous of another girl — a "sneaky, stuck-up, two-faced gossip who thinks she's so grown-up" — because this girl had Jacque "under her spell."

As for Jacque, she said of Anne years later, "I thought she was a little spoiled, but I don't think she thought so herself."

"There's a lot to be said about the boys," Anne told her diary, but added, "or maybe not so much after all." She went down a laundry list of boys in her class. Maurice was "one of my many admirers, but pretty much of a pest." And "Rob Cohen used to be in love with me too, but I can't stand him anymore. He's an obnoxious, two-faced, lying, sniveling little goof who has an awfully high opinion of himself." Herman had "a filthy mind," Jopie was "a terrible flirt and absolutely girl-crazy." Harry was nice — "the most decent boy in our class."

Anne got another one of her fevers toward the end of June and missed school. All her friends came over with homework and the latest news. Anne also got a visit from Kitty, whom she hadn't seen in years — the girl who had drawn such beautiful pictures in school and who sometimes had drawn pictures for Anne's stories when they were older. Once Anne got interested in boys and movie stars, Kitty got less interested in Anne. But that day, Kitty found Anne different — more thoughtful.

On June 20, Anne again told her diary that "I don't have a friend." She knew she had a loving family and plenty of kids she could joke around with and "a throng of admirers who can't keep their adoring eyes off me and who sometimes have to resort to using a broken pocket mirror to try and catch a glimpse of me." In short, Anne had everything but "my one true friend," someone to whom she could say "things that lie buried deep in my heart."

This was what her diary was going to be. A friend named Kitty.

Over the more than fifty years since Anne's diary was published, people have wondered if Kitty was the schoolgirl Anne had known. Or maybe she came from a character in a novel — Anne and Jacque loved acting out scenes from books about a girl named Joop who had a best friend named Kitty.

However the name Kitty reached Anne, and it may have been plucked out of the air, Kitty stood for a part of Anne that could open up and that she was just getting to know. With Kitty, she could show herself to herself, like a mirror that reflected not just the surface but what she looked like deep inside, far below.

From then on, all of Anne's diary entries were addressed to Kitty, as though each were a personal letter. And she signed off, "Yours, Anne M. Frank." Or simply, "Yours, Anne."

§§

The first weeks of Anne's life as a teenager were busy and happy. She wrote in her diary about a group of five girls who played Ping-Pong, who called themselves The Little Dipper Minus Two. (They had originally thought the constellation had only five stars and changed the name after realizing it actually had seven.) After Ping-Pong, they went out for ice cream and always found boys to pay for them. Anne admitted to being at a "tender age" for boys, but also took great pride in saying that once she and a boy "get to talking, nine times out of ten I can be sure he'll become enamored on the spot."

She wasn't bragging. Hello Silberberg, a good-looking sixteen-year-old boy, met Anne that June and was completely enchanted with her. His real name was Helmuth — Hello was a nickname, not a way of saying hi. He'd just broken up with Ursula, a girl his own age, a girl Anne knew and called "perfectly sweet and perfectly boring." Anne was happy to say that since Hello had met Anne, he realized he'd been "falling asleep" with Ursula. "So I'm kind of a pep tonic," Anne wrote. "You never know what you're good for!"

Hello didn't mind that Anne was only thirteen. "People often ask the question," he said years later, "sixteen-year-old boy being interested in a thirteen-year-old girl? It happens. She was fascinating."

But Anne was already in love with Peter Schiff, another sixteen-year-old. When Peter said hello to her, she was thrilled, even though he hadn't spoken to her in a long time. "I love Peter as I've never loved anyone," Anne wrote. "I tell myself he's only going around with all those other girls to hide his feelings for me." Or maybe, Anne thought, Peter was assuming that Hello and Anne were in love. Not so, Anne wrote: "He's just a friend."

Hello had come from Germany in 1938, just after *Kristallnacht*. At twelve, he had come alone — his parents never made it to Holland, only as far as Belgium. It made Anne sad that Hello hadn't seen his parents for four years. But Hello didn't seem sad. He was cheerful and told funny stories and even drove a car.

Otto liked Hello but got upset when Hello brought Anne home at ten minutes past eight one night. The curfew for Jews was eight. Otto was very much afraid — he and Edith knew things they weren't sharing with their children: that Jews were being rounded up for any offense (breaking curfew could get you arrested and jailed); that some Jews were getting summonses assigning them to work camps in Germany; that all Jews, eventually, would be made to leave Holland and, if the rumors were true, would be sent to their death.

⁋⁋

Anne's report card that year wasn't bad: "one D, a C– in algebra and all the rest B's." Otto and Edith were unusual in that they didn't care much about grades. "As long as I'm healthy and happy and don't talk back too much, they're satisfied," Anne wrote. As for Margot's report card, Anne wrote, "Brilliant, as usual."

On Sunday, July 5, a meltingly hot summer day, Anne told her diary that a few days earlier her father had mentioned — out of nowhere, it seemed, during a walk around the square — the possibility of the family going into hiding. This would mean living a life that would be "cut off from the rest of the world" until the war ended. Anne had heard of such people — they were called *onderduikers*, or divers, by the Dutch, because they disappeared from their own lives as completely as if diving into a deep ocean and not surfacing again.

Anne had asked Otto why he was talking about this now.

"Well, Anne," he told her, "you know that for more than a year we've been bringing clothes, food and furniture to other people. We don't want our belongings to be seized by the Germans. Nor do we want to fall into their clutches ourselves."

When Anne got scared because "he sounded so serious," he told her not to worry. "Just enjoy your carefree life while you can," he said.

Writing about this talk with her father on Sunday afternoon while sunbathing on her roof, Anne wished, "Oh, may these somber words not come true for as long as possible."

It was almost three o'clock. The doorbell rang.

Anne couldn't have heard the bell, but someone — her mother or sister — must have called up to her. She'd been expecting Hello, only not until later.

Anne jotted down, "The doorbell's ringing, Hello's here, time to stop."

It wasn't Hello.

PART TWO:
The Secret Annex

For Edith Frank, it must have been a world-shattering moment. When she answered the door, a mailman gave her a letter from the Central Office for Jewish Emigration. She may have thought, at first, that Otto was about to be sent to a concentration camp.

But the letter was for Margot.

Margot had to go to the Central Office and then get on a train for Westerbork — a Dutch transit camp. This meant a holding place until you were sent out of the country to a work camp, which was really a concentration camp. She was supposed to pack her own sheets and blankets, and food for three days.

Otto wasn't home. Edith told Margot that the letter was for Otto and that she was going out. She went to the home of Hermann van Pels, Otto's partner, and told the girls not to answer the door for anyone.

"I was stunned," Anne wrote in her diary on hearing the news about her father. But Anne and Margot reassured themselves with something Pim had told them many times — the family would never split up.

When Hello came for Anne, no one answered the bell. In her diary, Anne said she could hear her mother and Hermann van Pels, who were now back, talking to Hello to send him home. But Hello remembered, years later, only silence at the door and his own disappointment.

In the privacy of their bedroom, Margot, who'd heard the truth, told Anne that the letter had been for her, not for their father. Anne started to cry. Bad enough to come after grown men — but sixteen-year-old girls? All over Holland, thousands of young people were sent such letters that weekend, and thousands of families were torn apart. Some teenagers wanted to go, thinking that work camps were

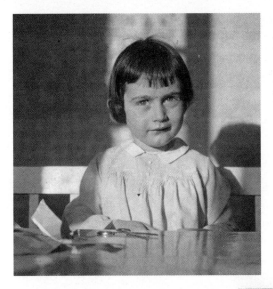

Anne Frank in the sunlight, age three. She was still living in Germany, but her family would soon flee Hitler's Nazi government and move to Holland.

Anne, all dressed up and about eight years old, checking her watch outside her father's office in downtown Amsterdam.

Anne loved dogs—and this one's name was Dopy. Anne was now ten years old.

Anne at school, age twelve, a year before she started writing her diary. She can be seen holding her pen in her unique grip, between her index and middle fingers.

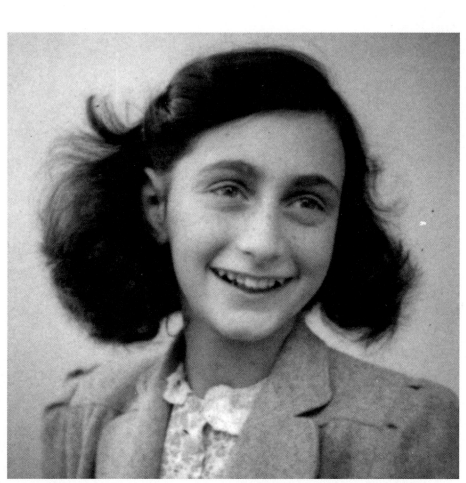

Anne just before her thirteenth birthday. She had a beautiful smile though she felt self-conscious about her slightly uneven teeth. Her family went into hiding a couple of months later.

A view of old downtown Amsterdam from the sky. The house where the Frank family hid, in the rooms Anne called the Secret Annex, is outlined in white. In front is a canal, and behind is the chestnut tree

Anne loved. The West Church (Westerkerk) with its tall clock tower can be seen on the right.

The bookcase on hinges that was specially built to hide the door that led to the Secret Annex.

The bedroom in the Secret Annex that Anne shared first with Margot and later with Dr. Pfeffer. The entire Annex was emptied when its residents were arrested. After the war, this room was temporarily refurnished so this photograph could be taken. It is empty again now, but the pictures Anne pasted to the wall are still there.

The kitchen, dining room, and living room that everyone in the Secret Annex shared was also the bedroom for Mr. and Mrs. van Pels. This room was also refurnished only temporarily and now stands empty.

A couple of early pages from Anne's diary. She wrote about her grandmother (whose snapshot is now missing) and stuck in a "marvelous letter" her father had written to her several years earlier. Anne thought this picture of herself, taken when she was twelve, was "horrible."

A street view of 263 Prinsengracht, the office building in front of the Secret Annex. This picture was taken many years after the war, when the whole building had become a museum that tells Anne's story and how it resonates throughout today's world.

actual work camps. I am strong! they told their parents, who refused to let them leave. Other teenagers were desperate to stay home, but their agonized parents insisted they leave, thinking that otherwise the whole family would be in danger.

At five, Otto came home. Now the whole family would discuss his plan. They, along with the Van Pelses, were to go into hiding. After nine years of life under Holland's intense and cloudy skies, they would submerge. They would become *onderduikers*, going below the ocean, not surfacing until it was safe to do so.

Otto and Edith had been arranging things for a year. They had planned to go into hiding on July 16. Now they had to go ten days early. During the spring, Otto had asked Miep if she'd be willing to help care for them and bring them food.

"Of course," Miep had answered instantly.

If she were found helping Jews, Otto reminded her, she, too, could be sent to a concentration camp.

"It was dangerous," Miep recalled years later. "It was my choice."

Where would they hide? Anne wanted to know. In the city, in the country, in a house, in a shack? Her father wouldn't say. But, he said, it would only be for a few weeks, maybe a few months.

They remained in hiding for twenty-five months.

That night, the family had to be careful. They had a tenant, a man in his thirties, who stayed up until ten o'clock. At eleven, Miep and her husband, Jan, came to take bags of belongings to the hiding place. Miep remembered that Anne's eyes "were like saucers, a mixture of excitement and terrible fright." Otto's idea was to casually leave a piece of paper, as if by accident, with an address in Switzerland on it. The tenant, and eventually everyone else, would assume the Frank family had gone to Switzerland.

Anne and Margot were told to pack their schoolbags with what mattered most to them.

The very first thing Anne packed was her diary. It was her way of taking herself with her — wherever it was she was going.

She then threw in hair curlers, handkerchiefs, books, a comb, and some old letters. "I stuck the craziest things in the bag," she wrote, "but I'm not sorry. Memories mean more to me than dresses." What upset her most was leaving Moortje behind. A note would be left, asking neighbors to take care of her. Though this was Anne's last night in her own bed, she fell asleep instantly.

§§

It was raining on the morning of July 6, a warm, steady rain typical of Dutch summers.

Edith woke Anne up at five-thirty. She got dressed in layers. Two undershirts, three pairs of underpants, a dress, a skirt, a jacket, a raincoat, two pairs of stockings, shoes, a cap, a scarf, "and lots more," Anne wrote. "It looked as if we were going off to spend the night in a refrigerator." This was their way of packing. Jews weren't allowed to travel or to change addresses, so they couldn't be seen with suitcases.

Margot left first, before seven-thirty, with Miep. She rode a bicycle, and she didn't wear her yellow Jewish star. Either one of these actions could have landed her in jail. "Margot was now like someone stunned," Miep remembered. They rode downtown, to the back house of Otto's office. This was the hiding place. Margot was supposed to wait upstairs, by herself, for the others. What a strange, unhappy time that must have been for her.

Shortly after Margot left, Anne and her parents

set off on foot. They got soaked. Their two-and-a-half-mile journey to the Old City took about an hour. Was Anne surprised that the hiding place was at 263 Prinsengracht, where she and Hanneli used to kid around? She wrote about it very matter-of-factly in her diary. She described every detail for Kitty — how you went up "ankle-twisting" staircases into a series of damp, neglected rooms. This was to be the world her family was diving into.

In her diary, Anne sounded like a tour guide, leading Kitty first through the two bottom floors. There was a large warehouse that ran uninterruptedly through the front and back buildings. The warehouse had a milling room for grinding cinnamon, cloves, and "pepper substitute" (in wartime, some real spices were impossible to get). Bep's father worked down there, and so did a couple of assistants who knew nothing of the people in hiding. Above them, on the second floor, the two houses divided. The front house had a big office on the canal — "very large, very light and very full," Anne wrote. Bep, Miep, and the bookkeeper, Mr. Kleiman, worked there. She next took Kitty through an alcove, which held the office safe, to a stuffy back room — the office of Mr. Kugler. He and Mr. Kleiman were running the businesses. Then they went through a narrow hallway into the back house and up four steps into Otto's private office —"the showpiece of the entire building," Anne described it. "Elegant mahogany furniture, a linoleum floor covered with throw rugs, a radio, a fancy lamp, everything first class." Next door was a large kitchen and a bathroom with hot water.

Up a flight of steps, and now Kitty was on the third-floor landing. The door on the left opened into storage rooms in the front house. The gray door to the right? That led to what Anne called the back house's Secret Annex. Miep, Miep's husband, Bep, Bep's father, Mr. Kleiman, and Mr. Kugler were all in on this secret, and each helped those in hiding stay hidden.

"No one would ever suspect there were so many rooms behind that plain gray door," Anne wrote. On the left, beyond a narrow hallway, was a room that became Otto and Edith's bedroom at night and a family room by day. On the right, in a room no wider than its window, was "the bedroom and study of the two young ladies of the family," Anne wrote.

These rooms, Miep recalled, had dark green wooden paneling and old, peeling, yellowing wallpaper. Up another flight of steep stairs was a room that surprised Anne — "such a large, light and spacious room in an old canal-side house like this." It had a stove and sink and became the kitchen, dining room, living room, and study for everyone by day, and the bedroom for Mr. and Mrs. van Pels at night. A tiny room next door was for their fifteen-year-old son, Peter. It had a ladder up to a large attic. "Now I've introduced you to the whole of our lovely Annex!" Anne told Kitty.

It was like a blink in time.

Anne became a teenager, ready to emerge into the world.

Anne was in hiding. Submerged.

§℘

A couple of months later, she wrote in the very front of her diary, "I am, Oh, so glad that I took you along." Miep had said that Anne spoke about her girlfriends as if each were her best and only friend. Anyone reading Anne's diary feels this way, too — as if the reader is Anne's best and only friend. Kitty was someone to tell everything to, and Anne was the girl who couldn't stop talking. She wrote — and wrote and wrote.

What is now called *The Diary of Anne Frank* started out with the cloth-covered diary she got on her thirteenth birthday. She filled that up in less than six months. Then she used school notebooks and office notebooks. When she was almost fifteen, she rewrote her entire diary up to that point, using thin sheets of blue and light pink tracing paper she got from the office and kept in a folder. She wrote on both sides of each page. The printed diary is nearly 350 pages long — and she didn't write in it every day, sometimes skipping entire weeks because she was ill and had to stay in bed. She wrote only in her room or in her parents' room and never when other people were there. She printed in circular letters, or used a rather tall, tilting, elegant script. She pasted in pictures of herself, with captions: "Gorgeous photograph isn't it!!!!" she wrote next to one. And, next to another, "This photograph is horrible and I look absolutely nothing like it." She spent 761 days in hiding, and she told exactly what it felt like, starting on the very first day.

ℰℰ

The place was a total mess, boxes piled up floor to ceiling, with all the stuff that had been brought to the Annex for months. Margot and Edith couldn't move. They were "tired, miserable and I don't know what else," Anne wrote. Anne and her father — "the two cleaner-uppers" — worked for hours, too busy even to stop to eat, unpacking, filling cupboards, sewing curtains to cover the windows, hammering nails, scrubbing floors. Trying to turn these musty rooms into a home. There was even some furniture from their apartment, things her mother had claimed had been taken in for repair. Anne made her room more cheerful by putting up pictures of movie stars and the children of the English and Dutch royal families; portraits of Leonardo da Vinci and Rembrandt; cutouts of cute babies and a picture of chimpanzees having a tea party; a photograph of a pink rose. "There's probably not a more comfortable hiding place in all of Amsterdam," Anne wrote. "No, in all of Holland."

She was right. Most families in hiding had to separate, because there wasn't enough room for all of them in any one place. Also, by splitting up, families lowered the risk of all of them being found out.

Some hiding places, such as the crawl space below the floorboards of a house, were so cramped that people couldn't even stand up straight. Some children were sent off to the countryside as "cousins" of Christian families. Many of the Dutch Jews who went into hiding survived — 16,000 out of 25,000. The other 9,000, which included Anne and her family, were captured sooner or later.

§§

The day after the Franks went into hiding, Hanneli went to their apartment to pick up a kitchen scale. "It was a beautiful day," Hanneli remembered, after all that rain the day before. She rang the bell a number of times. Finally, the tenant came to the door.

"Don't you know that the entire Frank family has gone to Switzerland?" he asked Hanneli.

Soon, all of Anne's friends heard this news. Hanneli went back to Anne's apartment, this time with Jacque. Anne's bed wasn't made, and her clothes were thrown all over. Her room had always been so neat.

§§

Hermann, Auguste, and Peter van Pels arrived at the hiding place a week after the Franks. The seven in hiding, who jokingly called their new home the "orphanage," fell into a routine that had rules as strict as any they'd had to put up with outside, under the Germans.

After working hours, they could make noise, but during working hours they had to whisper, walk around in stocking feet, not use a faucet or flush a toilet — be "as still as baby mice," Anne wrote. Who would have guessed, she asked Kitty, "that quicksilver Anne would have to sit so quietly for hours on end, and what's more, that she could?" Even though there were a number of helpers downstairs, there were always people in the office who didn't know and must never find out. The only way to get rid of trash and garbage was to burn everything in the stove, down to the tiniest potato peel, because anything left in a trash can might be noticed. "One small act of carelessness and we're done for!" Anne wrote, summing up the terror that never really left them, not for a moment.

They all had to be out of bed by seven on workdays. Blackout paper, heavy as cardboard, which got put up every night, came down. One by one, each person used a small, cold-water bathroom outside the Franks' bedroom. Everyone had to be dressed and ready by eight-thirty, with beds pushed back and tables brought out.

Early in the day, Miep would appear. This was always a hard moment for her. It began with a silence, when these seven people — with all their needs and fears — would look at her, look to her.

Anne was the one to break the silence, rushing up with what Miep called a "rapid-fire barrage of questions": "Hello, Miep! What's going on? What is the news? Have you heard the latest? What's in the bag?" and "What about Moortje?" Anne missed her cat terribly — "my weak spot," Anne called her. Her eyes filled with tears whenever she thought about her cat. "And my clothes, my things — did you bring any of my things to me from home, Miep? Did you, Miep?" And she asked about friends. "Have any of them gone into hiding like us?" Jacque lived across the street from Miep. Was there any word of her?

Miep also had to deliver the news of the world, news that was like one of those changeable Dutch skies that only kept getting darker. By the end of July, 6,000 Jews had left Holland for concentration camps. And Jews who remained were no longer citizens, which meant they now had no rights at all.

As for food, there were three hundred pounds of beans, and barrels of potatoes, and cans of fish, fruit, and vegetables. They also had oatmeal and rice, and Hermann van Pels made salami using spices from the warehouse. Every day Bep brought them milk; Mr. Kleiman got them bread; and Miep was responsible for the rest, meat and fresh vegetables. She went to several different shops, including a butcher friend of Hermann's. In the weeks before he went into hiding, Hermann had taken Miep to this butcher, telling her to simply stand beside him while he shopped. Once in hiding, Hermann told Miep to go back to the butcher and give him a list. When the butcher saw her, he gave her as much meat as he could. And not a word was spoken.

Bep's father built a bookcase to block the plain gray door. "It swings out on its hinges and opens like a door," Anne wrote. Empty black-and-white bound account books filled the shelves. This created the wonderful illusion that there was no gray door and nothing beyond it — no secret rooms, no people in hiding. Years later, Otto spoke of how much it had meant to all of them that his employees "proved to be sacrificial helpers and genuine friends in a time when bad powers had the upper hand."

Mr. Kleiman brought them books, and Miep took out five library books once a week. Anne, Margot, and Peter did homework every morning. They studied languages, history, science, geometry, and geography. Otto gave out the assignments and checked them. Margot worked tirelessly. Anne, in the course of a day, might study coffee-growing in Brazil, Old World and New World monkeys, the number of toes on a hippopotamus, Bible stories, "and then a comparison between the Mississippi and the Missouri!"

And she always put up a fuss about her worst subject. "I simply refuse to do that wretched math every day," she wrote. Peter needed a lot of extra help, and Otto was happy to give it to him. Anne and Margot studied shorthand through a correspondence course Bep had signed up for. The adults did chores, such as scraping carrots or peeling potatoes, and read and knitted.

At twelve-thirty they took a break. All the workers downstairs went out for an hour and a half, and any one of the helpers who had the time would come up for lunch and a visit. The long hours of the afternoon were spent much like the morning — reading, studying, napping, doing kitchen chores, and speaking in whispers. Since the windows always had to be covered, with curtains by day and blackout paper at night, the rooms got very stuffy in the summer and so hot the butter would melt.

At the end of the workday, one of the helpers came up to say that all the other workers had gone home. The seven in hiding went downstairs to Otto's old private office on the second floor and gathered around the radio. They listened to news broadcasts from England. News on other stations was controlled by the Germans. Otto and Hermann caught up with how the business was doing. Anne and Margot did stretches and exercises. Sometimes they danced. Miep and Bep left the girls some office chores, mostly to give them something to do. They also listened to classical music on the radio (Anne loved Mozart), played board games such as Monopoly, and recited poetry.

Bath time was a lovely part of the evening, the chance to use real hot water from the office kitchen and sit in a wooden washtub. Anne carried the tub into the big office bathroom. "I can sit down, turn on the light, lock the door, pour out the water without anyone's help, and all without the fear of being seen," Anne wrote.

Bedtime began at nine with "an enormous hustle and bustle," Anne wrote. Chairs were moved back, beds pulled out, sheets and blankets unfolded — "nothing stays where it is during the daytime." They went to bed around ten. Anne slept on a small daybed, so short that chairs had to be put under her head to make it longer.

Up in the attic, Miep remembered, were barrels of potatoes, and laundry hanging up to dry, and a little woodworking shop where Peter tinkered with tools. And two windows that were to become very important to Anne. One showed her the chestnut tree in the courtyard. Anne spent hours gazing at that tree, watching its leaves fall and return as the seasons passed. The other window had a skylight that, when opened, offered "the only breath of fresh air," according to Miep. It faced the top half of the Westerkerk clock tower, so big and so close you could almost touch it. Bells tolled, chimes sounded every quarter hour, and whole songs rang out on the weekends. Anne told Kitty that Margot and her parents found it overpowering. "Not me," Anne wrote.

"I liked it from the start; it sounds so reassuring, especially at night."

So this was Anne's life — a few rooms with too little air, a chiming clock tower, a leafy tree, and only a tiny piece of the immense Dutch sky. For her, it was both a prison and a cocoon. She was trapped, but she was growing and developing. She wasn't alone, of course, with everyone practically on top of one another. And her relationships with everyone else went through changes as the days and months went by, especially when it came to Peter van Pels.

Miep thought Peter, with his thick dark hair and dreamy blue eyes, was good-looking and sweet. Anne was not so impressed at first. She presented him to Kitty as "a shy, awkward boy whose company won't amount to much." A week later she wrote, "He's an obnoxious boy who lies around on his bed all day. . . . What a dope!" Peter had brought his cat along, though he'd been told not to. Mouschi was a skinny black cat that scared Anne a little.

"One big family," Anne described them all. A family that often didn't get along. Mrs. van Pels had vicious fighting matches with her husband. "I've never seen anything like it," Anne wrote. "Mother and Father wouldn't dream of shouting at each other like that." Both Van Pelses felt free to rip into Anne. "They criticize everything, and I mean everything, about me: my behavior, my personality, my manners; every inch of me, from head to toe and back again," Anne wrote. She asked herself if she was really as bad-mannered, headstrong, stubborn, pushy, stupid, and lazy as the Van Pelses said she was. "No, of course not," she answered.

"You should have been at our house," Mrs. van Pels told Anne, "where children were brought up the way they should be." But even Otto thought they were terrible parents. "They were absolutely no good" for Peter, he said years later. "Peter didn't have the backing of his parents at all."

It irritated Anne when Mrs. van Pels tried to flirt with Otto. "She pats him on the cheek and head, hikes up her skirt and makes so-called witty remarks in an effort to get Pim's attention. Fortunately, he finds her neither pretty nor charming." Before their time in hiding, Edith and Mrs. van Pels had been friendly but not close. Now Edith found her "too stupid for words." But this wasn't something Anne and her mother could team up on. "I simply can't stand Mother," Anne wrote of their own ever-worsening relationship. "I don't know why I've taken such a terrible dislike to her." Anne felt smothered by Edith — or ignored. "I have to be my own mother," she decided.

At a time when any teenage girl would want to break away from her mother, physically and emotionally, Anne, of course, couldn't get more than a few steps away. They were together every moment of every day and every night, for weeks and months and years.

As for Margot, sometimes they were "the best of buddies" — and then Anne would write, "Margot's a stinker (there's no other word for it), a constant source of irritation, morning, noon and night."

One evening, while eating "mothball cookies" (molasses cookies that were stored in a closet full of mothballs), Mrs. van Pels asked Anne if she could learn to love Peter like a brother.

"Oh, no!" Anne answered, while thinking, "Oh, ugh!"

Still, Anne was warming up to Peter. "From time to time," Anne wrote, "Peter can be very amusing." They both liked to dress up. One night, he put on one of his mother's skintight dresses and Anne wore one of Peter's suits. "The grown-ups split their sides laughing," Anne told Kitty, "and we enjoyed ourselves every bit as much." That fall, Peter had to move sacks of beans from hooks in the hallway up to the attic. He'd gotten five of the six fifty-pound sacks upstairs when the last one broke — "and a flood," Anne wrote, "or rather a hailstorm, of brown beans went flying through the air," making enough of a racket "to raise the dead." Peter, shocked, saw Anne standing there at the bottom of the stairs, "like an island in a sea of brown, with waves of beans lapping at my ankles." He laughed and laughed. Luckily, this wasn't heard by anyone who might grow suspicious.

A constant worry in the Annex was of someone getting sick with something far worse than Anne's recurring fevers. One day Otto was covered with spots and had a high temperature. "It looks like measles," Anne wrote. "Just think, we can't even call a doctor!" Fortunately, he recovered. Any interruption in the day-to-day routine added to the tension and danger. When a plumber came to work on the pipes downstairs, the people in hiding had to "sit still all day and not say a word," Anne wrote. Not even whisper. Not even walk to the bathroom (they had to use canning jars). Another time, people in the Annex thought a carpenter was about to discover their hiding place. "My hand's still shaking, though it's been two hours since we had the scare," Anne wrote. This kind of fear was as much a part of daily life as the loneliness and crowding and boredom.

Still, they knew how lucky they were. "Our many Jewish friends and acquaintances are being taken away in droves," Anne wrote. She mentioned the dreary conditions at Westerbork, the transit camp where Jews were held: "The people get almost nothing to eat, much less to drink . . . women and children often have their heads shaved." The radio reported that Jews in concentration camps were being killed with poison gas. *Perhaps that's the quickest way to die,* Anne thought.

୫୭

"We had lots of fun on Monday," Anne wrote in late October. "Miep and Jan spent the night with us."

Anne and Margot slept in their parents' room, and Miep "climbed into Anne's hard little bed," she remembered, "which was very toasty with blanket upon blanket, so many blankets." She heard all the nighttime sounds in the Annex, "coughing, the squeak of springs, the sound of a slipper dropping beside a bed, the toilet flushing, Mouschi landing on his padded feet somewhere above me." And the booming Westertoren clock. Though she worked right downstairs, she'd never heard the clock so loud.

She didn't sleep at all. She didn't even close her eyes. "The fright of these people who were locked up here was so thick I could feel it pressing down on me," Miep said. "For the first time I knew what it was like to be a Jew in hiding."

The next morning Anne, of course, was full of questions: "How did you sleep? Did the ringing of the Westertoren clock keep you awake? Could you hear the noise of planes on their way to bomb Germany? Could you sleep through all that?" Miep tried not to let on how difficult her "long fright-filled night" had been. But Anne could see. "Anne had a look of satisfaction on her face," Miep said. "It was not spoken, but we both knew that I had briefly crossed over from outsider to insider."

Anne looked different. She put on nineteen pounds in her first three months in hiding and grew four inches that first year. You can get to know the teenage Anne vividly during this time through her diary, but you can't ever see the person who wrote it. All the many photographs of Anne were taken when she was still a girl and before she went into hiding.

"Anne thought her best feature was her thick, shining dark brown hair," Miep remembered, hair that was nearly black. She combed it several times a day, always covering her shoulders with what Miep described as "a triangular shawl of fine cotton, beige with pink, light green, and blue roses and other small figures on it." Every night Anne set her hair in pin curls. Margot, too, curled her hair. Anne also manicured her nails and bleached her upper lip.

During that rainy, chilly, gloomy fall, Miep noticed changes in the others, too. Edith, now forty-two years old, was growing "dismal," Miep said. Even when the radio reported good news in the war against Germany, Edith "saw no light at the end of the tunnel." Edith, in Holland, had been homesick for Germany. Now she must also have felt homesick for the life they'd just left behind. Homesick twice over.

Whenever Jewish families were forced to leave their homes, a truck from the Puls company would come and take out all their belongings. By chance,

Miep saw the Van Pelses' home emptied — "pulsed," as it was called. When Miep mentioned it, Mrs. van Pels broke down in tears. After that, Miep tried not to deliver bad news, although Anne always sensed when Miep was holding something back. "She'd pull and squeeze, probe and stare me down, until I'd hear myself revealing just what I had decided not to reveal," Miep said. "Anne would have made a great detective."

ՏՑ

"Great news!" Anne told Kitty in November. "We're planning to take an eighth person into hiding with us!"

It was Miep's idea. Dr. Frederick Pfeffer, known as Fritz, was Miep's dentist, and someone the Franks knew from their old Saturday afternoon get-togethers. It was typical of Miep to keep seeing this "lovely, lovely man," as she called him, and pay no attention to the law that only Jews could see Jewish doctors.

Dr. Pfeffer was astonished when he arrived at the hiding place. Hadn't the Franks fled the country? He "looked as if he were going to keel over," Miep said.

Strangely, Dr. Pfeffer moved into Anne's room, and Margot went to sleep in her parents' room. Now Anne had a fifty-three-year-old male roommate — a situation that soon became extremely irritating to both of them. Less than two weeks later, Anne described Dr. Pfeffer as "an old-fashioned disciplinarian and preacher of unbearably long sermons on manners." Miep had to admit that Dr. Pfeffer's "stuffy ways" definitely got on Anne's nerves. Anne never knew much about Dr. Pfeffer — including the fact that he had a fifteen-year-old son living in London.

The winter days were short. It didn't get light until nine and by four-thirty it was dark again. Miep noticed more changes in the Annex. By the end of 1942, "Some of the spirit had gone out of the people upstairs," she said. The relationship between Edith and Mrs. van Pels was visibly "starchy." One day Edith snapped — at *Mr.* van Pels — "I can't stand that stupid chatter of yours a minute longer." Peter spent more and more time by himself in the attic. Anne's coloring had become pale and pasty. Margot, Miep said, "could sit in one place endlessly."

Dr. Pfeffer kept telling Anne to *shh, shh*, all day long. He also shushed her at night whenever she turned over in bed or jiggled the chairs beneath her head. "Really," Anne told Kitty, "it's not easy being the badly brought-up center of attention of a family of nitpickers. . . . Everyone thinks I'm showing off when I talk, ridiculous when I'm silent, insolent when I answer, cunning when I have a good idea, lazy when I'm tired, selfish when I eat one bite more than I should, stupid, cowardly, calculating, etc., etc. . . . I'm stuck with the character I was born with, and yet I'm sure I'm not a bad person. I do my best to please everyone, more than they'd ever suspect in a million years."

Sometimes, when the office was closed, Anne would sit downstairs and peer through a chink in the curtains. And she was deeply affected by what she could see of the world outside. Children, with "no coats, no socks, no caps and no one to help them. Gnawing on a carrot to still their hunger pangs." Every night Germans cruised the streets and arrested as many Jews as they could. "In the evenings when it's dark," she wrote, "I often see long lines of good, innocent people, accompanied by crying children, walking on and on, ordered about by a handful of men who bully and beat them until they nearly drop." She said, "I feel wicked sleeping in a warm bed, while somewhere out there my dearest friends are dropping from exhaustion or being knocked to the ground. . . . And all because they're Jews."

In direct contrast to the world, Anne's writing continued to grow more beautiful. Out the window, she could see a houseboat, where a captain lived with his family. "He has a small yapping dog," Anne wrote. "We know the little dog only by its bark and by its tail, which we can see whenever it runs around the deck. . . . By now I can recognize the women at a glance: gone to fat from eating potatoes, dressed in a red or green coat and worn-out shoes, a shopping bag dangling from their arms, with faces that are either grim or good-humored, depending on the mood of their husbands."

"Guess what's happened to us now?" Anne wrote in February 1943. And it was a real cause for worry. The owner of 263 Prinsengracht had sold the buildings without telling any of the office workers. When the new owner showed up to inspect the entire place, the people downstairs said they didn't have the key to the top floors. The new owner let it go, but Anne was afraid he'd return, demanding to see the Annex. "In that case, we'll be in big trouble!" she wrote. Miep was scared, too. "This new owner could do anything he wanted," she said.

Anne's fears got worse at night. She had a vision of Hanneli: "I saw her there, dressed in rags, her face thin and worn," she told Kitty. "She looked at me with such sadness and reproach in her enormous eyes." Anne was getting dark circles under her eyes because she slept so fitfully. Hundreds of Allied planes (British and American) passed over Holland to bomb Germany, and German anti-aircraft guns fired away at them. These guns were "booming away until dawn," she wrote, making "so much noise you can't hear your own voice." She crawled into her father's bed nearly every night for comfort. She sounded a little embarrassed about this, but told Kitty, "wait till it happens to you!" One night, Anne begged her father to light a candle, but he refused. After another burst of anti-aircraft fire, Edith leaped out of bed and lit a candle, much to Otto's anger. "After all, Anne is not an ex-soldier!" Edith declared, defending her daughter's right to be terrified.

In March, everyone thought burglars had broken in downstairs. Nothing was missing, but what if someone had noticed chairs grouped around the radio, a radio tuned to England?

By that summer, everything was in short supply. They had to use paper that strawberry recipes were printed on for toilet paper. The only shampoo was "a very sticky liquid cleanser," as Anne described it, making hair washing "no easy task." Combing out wet hair was also difficult because the family comb had only ten teeth left. Synthetic soap didn't leave bathers feeling clean and left a gray film on the water.

The food, Anne wrote, was now "terrible." Lunch was "either spinach or cooked lettuce with huge potatoes that have a rotten, sweetish taste. If you're trying to diet, the Annex is the place to be!" They had to spend hours rubbing mold off beans before they could be eaten. "The kitchen smells like a mixture of spoiled plums, rotten eggs and brine," Anne told Kitty. "Ugh, just the thought of having to eat that muck makes me want to throw up!" Anne later referred to "food cycles" — which meant eating one particular food until it ran out. It could be cucumbers, tomatoes, or endive — "Endive with sand, endive without sand," she wrote. Another time it was sauerkraut. Not much fun, Anne said, to eat sauerkraut every day for lunch and dinner — "but when you're hungry enough, you do a lot of things," she said.

It infuriated Anne to find bread, cheese, jam, and eggs in Dr. Pfeffer's cupboard. This was "absolutely disgraceful," she wrote, from a man they'd "treated with such kindness and whom we took in to save from destruction." He was "slipping lower and lower" in her estimation, "and he's already below zero."

Anne later spoke about how they'd all heard one another's stories a thousand times. "It all boils down to this," she wrote, "whenever one of the eight of us opens his mouth, the other seven can finish the story for him. We know the punch line of every joke before it gets told, so that whoever's telling it is left to laugh alone."

§§

"Little Anne," Miep said, "was turning into not-so-little Anne before our very eyes. She was simply bursting out of her clothes, and her body was changing shape as well." Forget buttons, Miep said, "It was impossible even to try to make buttons meet." Her undershirts were so tiny they didn't cover her stomach. "She had arrived a girl," Miep said, "but she would leave a woman."

Miep thought that sometimes Anne felt pretty and sometimes she felt ugly. Miep came across a pair of high-heeled burgundy leather pumps, secondhand but in good condition, which she gave to Anne. "Never have I seen anyone so happy," Miep remembered.

Anne, who always chattered a mile a minute, got very quiet, chewed her lip, and walked across the room in her new shoes, back and forth, more and more steadily.

Miep tried to make Anne's fourteenth birthday special, buying "little sweets and goodies, books, blank paper, secondhand things." Anne especially liked a big book on her favorite subject, Greek and Roman mythology. Books were growing more important to Anne. "If I'm engrossed in a book, I have to rearrange my thoughts before I can mingle with other people," she told Kitty. She clearly appreciated Miep and the other helpers, writing that "others display their heroism in battle or against the Germans, our helpers prove theirs every day by their good spirits and affection."

There was a real burglary downstairs in July. The petty-cash box was stolen, along with coupons that could be used to buy sugar. And an Allied plane was shot down and crashed nearby. There was a terrible explosion and fires that could be seen from the Annex. "Anxiety was reaching such a pitch," Miep said of the people upstairs, "it left them drained and sick for days afterward."

And so ended Anne's first year in hiding.

"Our dearly beloved Westertoren bells have been carted off to be melted down for the war," Anne wrote in the summer of 1943. She found it unsettling, life without the bells. But that summer she began writing short stories — "something I made up from beginning to end," she told Kitty about her first story, "and I've enjoyed it so much that the products of my pen are piling up." She rewrote each story many times before copying it into a large ledger book she called *Stories and Events from the Secret Annex*. That first story was about a girl named Kitty who had a small black cat.

In one of her fables, a wise old dwarf locks a boy and a girl in a small cabin for four months. The girl is too carefree, the boy too serious. After their time together, the dwarf tells them they have both been changed, balanced, completed. They'd had to "make the best of having to live together." Anne, who never read her diary to the others, occasionally read her stories aloud and loved it if a story turned out to be "a big hit" with her audience. She wondered if she could publish her fairy tales under a pen name.

In September, Italy, Germany's main partner in the war, surrendered to the Allies. The people in hiding were thrilled — and had new hope the war might be over soon. Despite this good news, "Relationships here in the Annex are getting worse all the time," Anne wrote. "We don't dare open our mouths at mealtime (except to slip in a bite of food), because no matter what we say, someone is bound to resent it or take it the wrong way." Sundays were the worst. "Outside, you don't hear a single bird, and a deathly, oppressive silence hangs over the house and clings to me as if it were going to drag me into the deepest regions of the underworld. . . . I wander from room to room, climb up and down the stairs and feel like a songbird whose wings have been ripped off and who keeps hurling itself against the bars of its dark cage. 'Let me out, where there's fresh air and laughter!' a voice within me cries."

Sometimes Anne felt "on top of the world" when she realized how fortunate she was to be safe and with her family, but, she wrote, "I long to ride a bike, dance, whistle, look at the world, feel young and know that I'm free." She was, quite simply, "a teenager badly in need of some good plain fun."

Just writing about it, she said, made her feel a little better.

"The grown-ups are such idiots!" Anne wrote. Margot had gotten much nicer, no longer treating Anne like "a little kid who doesn't count," but Anne's feelings toward her mother grew even harsher. "I can't look lovingly into those cold eyes," Anne wrote. "If she had even one quality an understanding mother is supposed to have, gentleness or friendliness or patience or *some*thing, I'd keep trying to get closer to her. But as for loving this insensitive person, this mocking creature — it's becoming more and more impossible every day!"

That winter, Miep noticed, "Mrs. Frank began to act oddly." When Miep was leaving, Edith would follow her to the back of the bookcase and stand there "with an expression of wanting in her eyes." But she wouldn't say a word. Miep began taking Edith aside to talk to her, away from the others. Edith spoke of her bottomless sadness. "Miep, I see no end coming," she said.

๛

"I saw my face in the mirror," Anne wrote in January 1944, "and it looked so different. My eyes were clear and deep, my cheeks were rosy, which they hadn't been in weeks, my mouth was much softer. I looked happy, and yet there was something so sad in my expression that the smile immediately faded from my lips." Anne had just had a dream about Peter Schiff, her first Peter, the boy she'd been in love with right before she went into hiding.

"The sun is shining," Anne told Kitty as the winter went on, "the sky is deep blue, there's a magnificent breeze, and I'm longing — really longing — for everything: conversation, freedom, friends, being alone. . . . I feel as if I were about to explode." She found herself wandering restlessly from room to room. "I don't know what to read, what to write, what to do."

And then she fell in love.

Peter van Pels — the other Peter — kept staring at Anne, and she felt, as she later put it, "as if a light goes on inside me." They began talking more. They confessed they hadn't liked each other at all, in the beginning. As in Anne's fable, he'd found her too unruly, she'd thought him too withdrawn. "I now have a better understanding of why he always hugs Mouschi so tightly," Anne wrote. "He obviously needs affection too," since "neither Peter nor I have a mother." He came to understand, as Anne put it, that "even the biggest pests also have an inner self and a heart."

They joked around. "The Jews have been and always will be the chosen people!" Peter remarked. "Just this once," Anne replied, "I hope they'll be chosen for something good!" They went to the attic together and looked out at "the bare chestnut tree glistening with dew, the seagulls and other birds glinting with silver as they swooped through the air, and we were so moved and entranced that we couldn't speak."

By late February, Peter Schiff and Peter van Pels "have melted into one Peter," she told Kitty. "From early in the morning to late at night, all I do is think about Peter." Writing in her storybook about him, she described his "wealth of fine brown curls" and "gray-blue eyes." Anne felt she finally had someone to open up to. "We told each other so much, so very much," she wrote in March, "that I can't repeat it all. But it felt good; it was the most wonderful evening I've ever had in the Annex."

Anne worried that Margot might be jealous and

want Peter for herself. "I think it's so awful that you've become the odd one out," Anne told Margot.

"I'm used to that," Margot answered — "somewhat bitterly," Anne described it.

Sometimes Anne and Margot wrote each other letters, even though they talked every day. "It's easier for me to say what I mean on paper than face-to-face," as Anne put it. Margot must have felt the same way. "I'm just sorry I haven't found anyone with whom to share my thoughts and feelings," Margot wrote, "and I'm not likely to in the near future. But that's why I wish, from the bottom of my heart, that you will both be able to place your trust in each other. You're already missing out on so much here, things other people take for granted." Anne said this fully demonstrated "Margot's goodness."

Now that she was in love, Anne felt a new kind of happiness. "Oh, when I think back to Saturday night," she wrote, "to our words, our voices, I feel satisfied with myself for the very first time; what I mean is, I'd still say the same and wouldn't want to change a thing, the way I usually do."

§§

April 15, 1944. Anne was fourteen years and ten months old. She told Kitty to remember this "red-letter day for me." She got her first kiss. "I was too happy for words," she wrote, "he gave me a kiss, through my hair, half on my left cheek and half on my ear."

It was a lovely spring outside, "not too hot and not too cold, with occasional light showers," Anne said, and the chestnut tree was in leaf and beginning to blossom. Peter and Anne kissed and kissed — "In a daze," she wrote, "we embraced, over and over again, never to stop, oh!"

But by the time she turned fifteen, Anne found herself drifting away from Peter. He was "still a child, emotionally no older than I am," was how she put it. She was afraid he wasn't capable of ever becoming a "friend for my understanding." In a jumble of feelings, she told Kitty, "Peter's a sweetheart, but I've slammed the door to my inner self; if he ever wants to force the lock again, he'll have to use a harder crowbar!" But then she asked, "Why does he hide his innermost self and never allow me access?"

He leaned on her too much, she said, and he didn't have a goal in life. Anne knew exactly what she wanted to do, in the near future and the far future. Spend a year in Paris and London, learn French and English, and study art history in a world filled with "gorgeous dresses and fascinating people," she said. She told Kitty that her "greatest wish is to be a journalist, and later on, a famous writer." Basically, she said, "I'm determined to write!"

For his part, Peter never stopped loving Anne. Peter had barely spoken to Miep for two years but approached her just before Anne's birthday. He gave her a few coins. Could Miep find some pretty flowers for Anne? "It's a secret, Miep," he said. "Of course," she told him. Miep could only find a few lavender peonies. Miep remembered that when she gave him the flowers, "red spots rose in his cheeks."

❧❧

"Which of the people here would suspect that so much is going on in the mind of a teenage girl?" Anne asked Kitty at one point. She told her father not to think of her in terms of her age — "since all these troubles have made me older."

"When I think back to my life in 1942, it all seems so unreal," she wrote in March 1944. "The Anne Frank who enjoyed that heavenly existence was completely different from the one who has grown wise within these walls." She looked back at that other Anne Frank as "a pleasant, amusing, but superficial girl, who has nothing to do with me." It had been hard for her, she said, after a life "filled with sunshine" and "years of being adored" to "adjust to the harsh reality of grown-ups and rebukes." The fights and the accusations, she said, "I couldn't take it all in." The only way she could keep her bearings was to talk back. The first half of 1943 brought much sadness "and the gradual realization of my faults and shortcomings." She felt left on her own to face the "difficult task" of improving herself, which she did "by holding my behavior up to the light and looking at what I was doing wrong." She admitted this was still only a "half-completed task." She realized, "Beauty remains, even in misfortune. If you just look for it, you discover more and more happiness and regain your balance."

Even her attitude toward the Van Pelses changed. They weren't "entirely to blame for the quarrels," she said. Like a Dutch sky, there were bits of blue and shades of gray in everyone.

Anne's moods swung like the pendulum of a clock (something she once compared herself to), and sometimes her thoughts swung, too, even while she was expressing them. "It's a wonder I haven't abandoned all my ideals, they seem so absurd and impractical," she wrote in July 1944. "Yet I cling to them because I still believe, in spite of everything, that people are truly good at heart." And in the same breath she wrote, "I see the world being slowly transformed into a wilderness, I hear the approaching thunder that, one day, will destroy us too, I feel the suffering of millions."

Just as Good Paula and Bad Paula were part of the same person, Anne also saw herself as "split in two." She was able to take a step back and "watch myself as if I were a stranger." In April 1944, she wrote, "Suddenly the everyday Anne slipped away and the second Anne took her place. The second Anne, who's never overconfident or amusing, but only wants to love and be gentle." No one knew her better side, she wrote in August. "Oh, I can be an amusing clown for an afternoon," she told Kitty, "but after that everyone's had enough of me to last a month." She was afraid people would make fun of the second Anne. "So the nice Anne is never seen in company," she explained. "I'm guided by the pure Anne within, but on the outside I'm nothing but a frolicsome little goat tugging at its tether."

"I've made up my mind to lead a different life from other girls," Anne wrote, "and not to become an ordinary housewife later on. What I'm experiencing here is a good beginning to an interesting life."

§§

Anne used Otto's old leather briefcase to store all the books and pages of her diary. Everyone in hiding knew this briefcase was off-limits. "The Franks believed in respecting the privacy of everyone, including children, and there was so little privacy in the hiding place," Miep said. "No one would dare to touch her papers or to read her words without her permission."

During the summer of 1944, Miep had an encounter with Anne she couldn't forget. Up until then, Anne had been "like a chameleon," as Miep described her, who would go "from mood to mood, but always with friendliness" and had always been "admiring and adoring" with her.

One day Miep saw Anne writing at a table by the window in her parents' room. The room was dark. Miep was almost on top of her before Anne noticed she was there. "I saw a look on her face at this moment that I'd never seen before," Miep said. "It was a look of dark concentration, as if she had a throbbing headache. This look pierced me, and I was speechless. She was suddenly another person there writing at the table."

Edith came into the room and spoke in German, a language she spoke only in tense situations. "Yes, Miep, as you know, we have a daughter who writes," she said.

Anne stood, shut her book, and said to Miep, "Yes, and I write about you, too." Miep said that Anne spoke "in a dark voice."

Miep was shaken. "It was as if I had interrupted an intimate moment in a very, very private friendship." Miep understood that "her diary had become her life."

From the beginning, when Anne had hoped her diary would be a source of comfort, this very private friendship only intensified. "I always wind up coming back to my diary — I start there and end there because Kitty's always patient," she wrote at one point. Some months later she wrote about how honest she'd always been with Kitty — "I've never shared my outlook on life or my long-pondered theories with anyone but my diary." In the spring of

1944, during another burglary downstairs, the people in hiding panicked. Someone suggested burning the radio — or Anne's diary. "Oh, not my diary," Anne wrote, "if my diary goes, I go too!"

§♣

On the radio one night in March 1944, a Dutch cabinet minister speaking from exile in London said that, after the war, diaries and letters would be collected and published to create a "picture of Holland's struggle for freedom." Right away Anne thought about using her diary as the basis for a novel called *The Secret Annex*. "The title alone," she said, "would make people think it was a detective story."

"Seriously, though," she added, "ten years after the war people would find it very amusing to read how we lived, what we ate and what we talked about as Jews in hiding."

She started rewriting her diary from beginning to end, at the rate of six pages a day, while still adding new entries. Sometimes she softened what she'd said about her mother and the others, now that she'd grown into a new awareness. "I soothe my conscience with the thought that it's better for unkind words to be down on paper than for Mother to have to carry them around in her heart," Anne wrote.

She changed the names of her "characters." The Van Pels family was now the Van Daan family. Miep and her husband, Jan Gies, became Anne and Henk van Santen (interesting, that Anne gave Miep her own name). For Dr. Frederick Pfeffer, Anne chose Albert Dussel, which translates to Albert Dope. Years later, Dr. Pfeffer's son called this name and the portrait of his father "a very large inaccuracy." Dr. Pfeffer was a man who loved life and loved sports, his son said, and to end up in a room was like "caging a bird."

❧❧

At this point in the war, many Dutch families were desperately poor and hungry. Burglaries and thefts were so common that Anne spoke of children as young as eight smashing the windows of people's homes and stealing whatever they could. "People don't dare leave the house for even five minutes," Anne wrote, "since they're liable to come back and find all their belongings gone."

There were two break-ins at 263 Prinsengracht that spring and summer. The worst of it was that some of the people in hiding might have been seen or heard. One night the police were called in and searched the buildings, getting as far upstairs as the bookcase. The office foreman had been suspicious of the goings-on at 263 Prinsengracht for some time. He'd found Hermann's wallet on the warehouse floor some months before. Anne and the others agonized over the burglaries, the careless moments.

In the late spring of 1944, war news got tremendously better. On D-Day, June 6, 1944, British, American, and Canadian troops landed on the beaches of Normandy, France, and began to push the Germans back. " 'This is *the* day,' " Anne wrote happily, in English, quoting the British radio. "The invasion has begun!" Otto posted a map of Europe on the wall, with many-colored pins showing the progress of the Allied forces. With each new victory, the pins got closer to Holland.

"Great news!" Anne wrote on July 21. "An assassination attempt has been made on Hitler's life." She cautioned herself against getting too excited about the possibility of Hitler's death, but she was ecstatic — "the prospect of going back to school in October is making me too happy to be logical! Oh dear, didn't I just get through telling you I didn't want to anticipate events? Forgive me, Kitty, they don't call me a bundle of contradictions for nothing!"

§§

Around ten-thirty on the morning of August 4, 1944, a Friday, Otto was in Peter's room helping him with his English. "But Peter," Otto said, "in English *double* is spelled with only one *b*!" Anne had been learning English, too. "Bad weather from one at a stretch to the thirty June," she wrote for Kitty. "Don't I say that well?"

It was hot; it smelled of pepper and thyme. Anne and Margot were reading. Downstairs, five men entered the warehouse. Four of them came into the office where Miep, Bep, and Johannes Kleiman, the bookkeeper, worked. "Sit still and not a word out of you!" one of them said. Miep looked up from her desk and saw that he was holding a gun.

Three of the men, Dutch Nazis, were in plain clothes. The fourth was in uniform. He was a German security police sergeant. These four went to the office of Victor Kugler, the business manager. "You have Jews hidden in this building," the Nazi in uniform said to Mr. Kugler. It wasn't a question.

For the last twenty-five months, Mr. Kugler, along with Mr. Kleiman, Miep, and Bep, had been providing everyone in the Annex with food, books, news, presents, and friendship. Now he had to take the Nazis upstairs.

Otto and Peter looked up from the English lesson to see a man pointing a gun at them. They put their hands up and went downstairs — to see Edith, Margot, Anne, and the Van Pelses all standing with their hands in the air. Margot was crying. Last to join them was Dr. Pfeffer, a gun at his back.

Karl Josef Silberbauer, the Nazi in uniform, asked where the valuables were kept. He found Otto's briefcase and turned it upside down. Anne's diary and all her loose pages tumbled to the floor. She had written her last entry three days earlier. Now she didn't even glance down. Silberbauer put money and jewelry into the empty briefcase. They were all told to pack.

Silberbauer noticed Otto's trunk, left over from his days as a German lieutenant in the First World War. But Otto Frank was a Jew. This seemed to up-set Silberbauer. He asked Otto how long they had been in hiding. "Two years and one month," Otto told him.

Silberbauer didn't believe it until Otto showed him pencil marks on the wallpaper, which recorded Anne's and Margot's growth over time.

Downstairs, Miep's husband, Jan, showed up around noon, as he always did. Before he could come inside, Miep ran to the door. "It's wrong here," she told him.

PART THREE:
A Piece of the Sky

❧

Miep and Bep weren't arrested, but Mr. Kugler and Mr. Kleiman were. The ten prisoners were put in a windowless truck and taken to security police headquarters. After the Nazis left, Miep and Bep gathered up the diary. Miep put the books and loose pages, unread, in the bottom drawer of her desk. "I'll keep everything safe for Anne until she comes back," she told Bep. She also kept Anne's combing shawl. "I still don't know why," she said decades later. Peter's cat, Mouschi, had disappeared during the arrest, but later showed up at the office, where Miep took care of him.

Someone had called the Nazi security police that

morning to report that there were Jews hiding in 263 Prinsengracht. The caller has never been identified. It could have been a neighbor. People who lived and worked nearby had thought there might be people in the Annex. Some were sure of it. Maybe one of the burglars had seen and said something. Other people thought it was the foreman who'd found Hermann's wallet. Others suspected a woman who cleaned the offices. A more recent theory blames a Dutch Nazi, a man Otto Frank had known before the war.

Mr. Kleiman and Mr. Kugler were sent to a Dutch prison camp. After several nights in jail, the Franks, the Van Pelses, and Dr. Pfeffer were taken by train to Westerbork, eighty miles north of Amsterdam. Anne was said to be glued to the window, gazing at fields and farm animals.

They spent the next month there. Anne had to work, breaking open batteries with a small chisel and separating the parts. She got so filthy, she looked like a coal miner. Men and women lived in separate barracks, but Anne could see her father and Peter at the end of the day. She was still lively and sweet, people said, not unhappy.

On September 3, they were all put on the last

train ever to leave Westerbork for Auschwitz, a death camp in Poland. The train ride, in cattle cars, took three days and two nights. On arrival, Otto was separated from his wife and children. He turned to see them for the last time. *I shall remember the look in Margot's eyes all my life,* he thought.

Many of those just off the train were gassed right away — if they were sick, if they were under fifteen, if they looked too old. Starvation and illness and overwork greeted those who were not immediately killed. Edith, Margot, and Anne had their heads shaved and had numbers tattooed on their left forearms. Everyone at the camp had lice. Anne also got a skin disease and had sores all over.

Anne, Margot, and Edith did not leave one another, not for a moment. Anne and her mother grew close, in this most terrible of places. A girl who'd known Anne at school saw her again at Auschwitz. "Her mother was someone against whom she rebelled," this girl remembered years later. "But in the camp, all of that actually completely fell away."

On October 28, Margot and Anne were sent to Bergen-Belsen, a German concentration camp, not officially a death camp. Edith stayed in Auschwitz and died there on January 6, 1945 — of hunger, exhaustion, and grief.

Anne's friend Hanneli, who'd already been sent to Bergen-Belsen, was shocked to find Anne there and not safe in Switzerland. She and Anne spoke through a barbed-wire fence filled with straw. "I couldn't see her," Hanneli said. "There wasn't much light. Maybe I saw her shadow." Anne said her parents were both dead; that Margot was very ill; that she was freezing, and hungry, and had lost her beautiful hair. Hanneli was able to pass a little food to her over the fence.

On January 27, 1945, Auschwitz was liberated by Russian troops. Otto Frank, who had survived, was now free. (And he began keeping a diary — a red notebook given to him by a Russian soldier.) Hanneli thought that if Anne had known her father was alive it might have given her strength. On April 15, Bergen-Belsen was liberated by British troops. Not many weeks before, Margot and Anne came down with typhus, a highly contagious disease that was spreading through the camp. Margot died somewhere between the end of February and the middle of March. Anne died a few days later.

❦

The Germans surrendered on May 8, ending the war in Europe. Six million Jews were dead, including a million and a half children. Holland's Jewish population was hit especially hard. There had been as many as 150,000 Jews in the country before the war. After it, only about 20,000 to 25,000 remained. Among Anne's friends, Hanneli, Kitty, Jacque, and Hello survived. Of the eight people hidden in the Annex, only Otto Frank survived. He later found Hanneli, who was now an orphan. "He became my father from then on," Hanneli said.

When Otto got back to Amsterdam in June, he found that Mr. Kleiman and Mr. Kugler had survived the prison camp. He went up to the empty rooms of the Annex (they had been "pulsed" after the arrest). He found three brown beans on the floor, left over from the day Peter's sack had split open. Otto kept the three beans for the rest of his life.

Otto learned of Edith's death from a friend. There was no news of Margot and Anne. June 12 was Anne's sixteenth birthday. Still no news. In July he found their names on a Red Cross list of the dead.

"Margot and Anne are not coming back," he told Miep. She opened her desk drawer and gave him the diary. "Here is your daughter Anne's legacy to you," she said.

§§

Otto was astounded. "I only learned to know her really through her diary," he said. "She never really showed this kind of inner feeling." And to Miep, "Who would have imagined what went on in her quick little mind?" Miep also admitted, "We did not know how intelligent she was."

After thinking it over, Otto decided to publish Anne's diary — to honor her memory, to grant her wish to be a published writer, and to share this war document with the world. He especially hoped young people would want to read it. He pieced together a version of the diary based on her original diary and her rewritten diary. He took out some parts he thought were too personal (those parts have since been put back in). A small number of copies were printed in Holland in 1947 with the title *Het Achterhuis* (*The House Behind*). It was published in America as *Anne Frank: The Diary of a Young Girl* in 1952 and became a phenomenal success.

A play about Anne opened in New York in 1955 and won a Pulitzer prize. Miep later saw the play in Amsterdam. "It was a very strange experience," she said. "I kept looking for my real friends to come on-stage." Anne, the girl who had daydreamed about going to Hollywood, was the subject of a 1959 Hollywood movie and, years later, a TV movie as well. *Anne Frank Remembered,* a documentary, won a 1996 Oscar. When the director accepted the award, Miep stood by his side. Miep was also knighted by the queen of Holland.

By the late 1950s, Otto's old office buildings stood empty. Otto Frank, along with other Dutch citizens, created the Anne Frank Foundation to preserve the buildings and turn them into a museum. The chestnut tree out back was dying, but it was saved. Following Otto's wishes, the foundation is also devoted to educating young people about the dangers of hatred and racism. Otto died in 1980 at the age of ninety-one. The foundation continues its work with children around the world.

§§

Schools and streets have been given her name. And just beyond Mars, there's an asteroid five miles across that circles the sun. As part of the celebrations marking the fiftieth anniversary of the end of the war, this asteroid was officially given the name Asteroid 5535 Annefrank. On June 13, 1944, Anne wrote in her diary, "The dark, rainy evening, the wind, the racing clouds, had me spellbound; it was the first time in a year and a half that I'd seen the night face-to-face." Now a piece of the sky has been named for her.

BIBLIOGRAPHY

BOOKS BY ANNE FRANK

Frank, Anne. *The Diary of Anne Frank: The Revised Critical Edition.*
Prepared by the Netherlands Institute for War Documentation. Edited by David Barnouw and Gerrold van der Stroom. Translated by Arnold J. Pomerans, B. M. Mooyaart-Doubleday, and Susan Massotty. New York: Doubleday, 2003. This book contains all of Anne's writings, including the different versions of her diary and the short stories and essays. There's also an in-depth analysis of the attacks on the authenticity of the diary (as part of the whole movement to deny the existence of the Holocaust), and how it was proven, without a doubt, to be genuinely Anne's words. There are chapters on the betrayal, the arrest, and the theatrical productions about Anne's life, and a brief biography. Quite simply, this eight-hundred-plus-page book has everything.

Frank, Anne. *The Diary of a Young Girl: The Definitive Edition.*
Edited by Otto H. Frank and Mirjam Pressler. Translated by Susan Massotty. New York: Anchor Books, 1996. This edition of the diary contains about thirty percent more material than the edition that was first published in 1947. Among other things, Anne reflects on the changes in her body and her growing sexuality.

Frank, Anne. *Anne Frank's Tales from the Secret Annex.*
Translated by Ralph Manheim and Michel Mok. New York: Bantam Books, 1994. Here are the fables, short stories, personal reminiscences, and essays. Anne's strong moral viewpoints on the wealthy and the poor, the powerful and the underprivileged can be heard.

BOOKS ABOUT ANNE FRANK

Adler, David A. *A Picture Book of Anne Frank.*
Illustrated by Karen Ritz. New York: Holiday House, 1994. Very good introduction to Anne's life for young readers.

The Anne Frank House. *Anne Frank in the World, 1929-1945.*
New York: Knopf, 2001. This excellent picture book puts Anne in the context of the changing political climate around her. The childhood photographs of Anne are especially moving.

Gies, Miep, with Alison Leslie Gold. *Anne Frank Remembered: The Story of the Woman Who Helped to Hide the Frank Family.*
New York: Simon & Schuster, 1988. Miep's lovely voice tells her own fascinating life story and how that life was linked to Anne's.

Lee, Carol Ann. *The Hidden Life of Otto Frank.*
New York: William Morrow, 2003. This writer, amazingly, has come up with new information on a subject that has already been written about extensively for decades.

Lindwer, Willy. *The Last Seven Months of Anne Frank.*
Translated by Alison Meersschaert. New York: Anchor Books, 1992. This harrowing, heartbreaking book is based on the author's documentary of the same title. Six women tell their stories, women who knew Anne at some point in her life. Among them is Hanneli Goslar, Anne's first friend in Holland.

Mueller, Melissa. *Anne Frank: The Biography.*
Translated by Rita and Robert Kimber. New York: Henry Holt, 1998.
This is an absolutely beautiful biography, far-reaching and thoughtful.

Van der Rol, Ruud, and Rian Verhoeven. *Anne Frank, Beyond the Diary, A Photographic Remembrance.*
Translated by Tony Langham and Plym Peters. New York: Puffin Books, 1995. A wonderful book with vivid pictures.

DOCUMENTARIES AND MOVIES

Anne Frank: The Whole Story.
Robert Dornhelm, director. Buena Vista Home Entertainment, 2001. Starring Ben Kingsley, Brenda Blethyn, Hannah Taylor Gordon, and Lili Taylor (as Miep Gies). Riveting movie based on Melissa Mueller's biography of Anne Frank. Very accurate telling of Anne's life, and the performances are wonderful.

Anne Frank: The Life of a Young Girl.
ABC News Productions for A&E Biography, 1998. This short, insightful documentary is part of Biography's Legendary Women series.

Anne Frank Remembered.
Jon Blair, writer, producer, and director. Narrated by Kenneth Branagh and Glenn Close. Sony Pictures Classics, 1995. Winner of an Academy Award for Best Documentary Feature. Fascinating study of Anne's life. Contains interviews with Miep Gies and Hanneli Goslar. Among many touching moments, Miep meets Dr. Pfeffer's son for the first time, and he thanks her for helping his father.

The Diary of Anne Frank.
George Stevens, director. Twentieth Century Fox, 1959. Starring Millie Perkins, Joseph Schildkraut, Shelley Winters, Richard Beymer, Gusti Huber, and Ed Wynn. Not altogether accurate, but this movie is still powerful and haunting. Shelley Winters won an Oscar for her portrayal of Mrs. van Pels.

MISCELLANEOUS

Alexander, Amir. "Stardust Delivers Surprising Images of Asteroid Annefrank."
The Planetary Society, November 5, 2002. This article describes the asteroid that was named for Anne Frank. http://planetary.org/html/news/articlearchive/headlines/2002/stardust_annefrank2.html

Calder, Simon, and Fred Mawer. *AAA Spiral Guides: Amsterdam.*
Heathrow, Florida: AAA Publishing, 2001. Excellent guidebook to Amsterdam, full of facts about the city's history and culture.

Duncan, Fiona, and Leonie Glass. *Eyewitness Top 10 Travel Guides: Amsterdam.*
New York: DK Publishing, 2003. Beautifully done guidebook to Amsterdam.

Fisher, Teresa. *Fodor's City Pack: Amsterdam.*
Third edition. New York: Fodor's Travel Publications, 2002. A small, informative guide to Amsterdam.

Knopf Guides: Amsterdam. Revised edition. New York: Knopf, 1994. Very thorough guidebook to Amsterdam, with glowing illustrations.

McDonald, George, and Brian Bell. *Insight Pocket Guide: Amsterdam.*
Second edition. Singapore: APA Publications, 2002. Very good overview of Amsterdam.

Royal Picture Gallery, The Hague. "Mauritshuis: Dutch Painting of the Golden Age."
New York: Metropolitan Museum of Art, 1984. Stunning paintings, including many images of the ever-changing Dutch sky.

University of Washington. "Flyby of Annefrank Asteroid to Help Stardust Prepare for Primary Mission."
Press release, October 28, 2002. An article about the asteroid Annefrank. http://www.spaceref.com/news/viewpr.html?pid=9656

Whiteley, Suzanne Mehler. *Appel Is Forever: A Child's Memoir.*
Detroit: Wayne State University Press, 1999. The author was born in Holland in 1935. She tells of the German occupation and her experiences in Bergen-Belsen with the pitch-perfect voice of a child.